SETTLING THE WEST

⌒ 1862 – 1890 ⌒

by Joanne Barkan

Table of Contents

Introduction

Imagine that you're living on a farm in Missouri in 1865. The long and brutal Civil War has finally ended. Your family is packing up to move. You are hoping to find more land and better opportunities. Where are you going? To the West.

The West was the area of land approximately between the Missouri River and the Sierra Nevada mountains.

It was a huge **territory**–about 1.2 billion acres. First came the Great Plains; then the Rocky Mountains. Finally, a huge desert stretched to the Sierra Nevada mountains. This vast area of grassy plains, rugged mountains, and parched deserts had several names. In 1865, some called this area the Wild West. Many simply called it "the West."

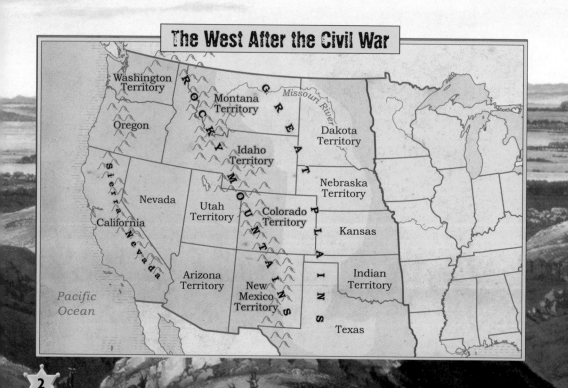

The West After the Civil War

Washington Territory
ROCKY
Montana Territory
GREAT
Missouri River
Oregon
Dakota Territory
Idaho Territory
Sierra Nevada
Nevada
Utah Territory
Colorado Territory
Nebraska Territory
California
Kansas
MOUNTAINS
PLAINS
Arizona Territory
New Mexico Territory
Indian Territory
Pacific Ocean
Texas

Before the Civil War, the West seemed terribly forbidding. Picture treeless **prairies**, snow-topped peaks, and barren sands. Could anyone really survive in the West? The answer is "Yes." Native Americans had lived there for thousands of years. Lone fur trappers had roamed the mountains since the early 1800s. Before 1858, a few prospectors had dug for gold. But only a few people chose to **settle**, or make their homes, there. During the 1840s and 1850s, tens of thousands of pioneers trekked across the West, but didn't stay. They didn't stop until they reached California or Oregon.

It's a Fact

If you looked at a map made before 1860, you'd probably find something odd. The Great Plains would likely be labeled the "Great American Desert." Some people then thought that the region was a wasteland. What a mistake! The Great Plains turned out to be some of the richest farmland in the world.

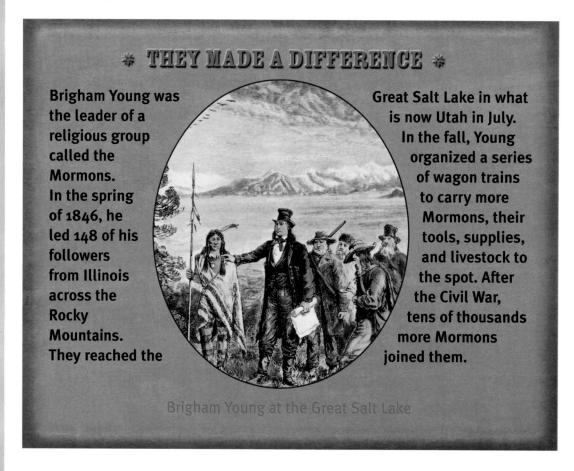

THEY MADE A DIFFERENCE

Brigham Young was the leader of a religious group called the Mormons. In the spring of 1846, he led 148 of his followers from Illinois across the Rocky Mountains. They reached the Great Salt Lake in what is now Utah in July. In the fall, Young organized a series of wagon trains to carry more Mormons, their tools, supplies, and livestock to the spot. After the Civil War, tens of thousands more Mormons joined them.

Brigham Young at the Great Salt Lake

After the Civil War, the West changed with amazing speed. Suddenly, people flocked to the area to make a new life. Why? Gold and silver **strikes** sparked their hopes. So did the amount of land that could be had for little or no money. New railroads made the long journey easier and spurred business. New inventions made farming the tough soil possible.

Congress passes the Homestead Act.	The Civil War ends. Millions of buffalo graze on the Great Plains.	Construction of the transcontinental railroad is completed.	Gold is discovered in the Black Hills.
1862	1865	1869	1875

After 1865, hundreds of thousands of settlers moved west almost every year. New towns sprang up, sometimes overnight. Settlers faced everything from grasshopper plagues to deadly battles over land. And the lives of Native Americans in the West changed forever as the area was settled. Read to find out more about the people who settled the West after the Civil War. Look for an answer to this question: Why would people risk so much to settle there?

gold mining in California

The Battle of Little Bighorn is fought.	An improved plow for cutting through sod is invented.	20,000 settlers claim land in one day in an Oklahoma land rush.	The Great Plains buffalo is near extinction.	The Battle of Wounded Knee is fought.
1876	1877	1889	1889	1890

The Early Settlers

Gold! After California's gold **rush** of 1849, few Americans expected to hear that magic word again. But in 1858, prospectors did find gold again. They struck gold near Pike's Peak at the eastern edge of the Rocky Mountains.

The rush was on! Within months, thousands of wagons rolled across the Great Plains to Pike's Peak in search of gold. "Pike's Peak or Bust!" became a popular slogan. Many gold-seekers scrawled it in huge letters on the sides of their wagons. As soon as they reached the foothills of the Rockies, the newcomers set up tents and shacks and got to work. They didn't find much gold that year. But businesses of all kinds sprang up in the mining camps.

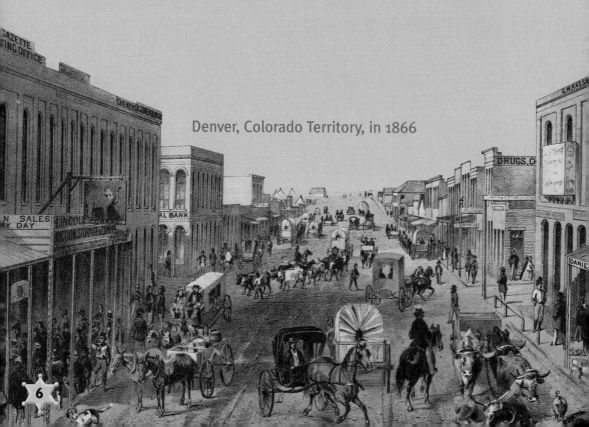

Denver, Colorado Territory, in 1866

Up went general stores, saloons, banks, blacksmith shops, and hotels to serve the miners. One of these mining camps became the great city of Denver. Today, Denver is the capital of Colorado.

Gold strikes produced gold rushes, and gold rushes often produced towns. This is what happened in what is now Nevada, Montana, and the Dakotas. When the gold ran out, some mining towns disappeared. But others grew into some of the western cities we know today, such as Butte (BYOOT), Montana.

In 1859, miners struck gold and silver again. This time the lucky spot was on the eastern slopes of the Sierra Nevada mountains. The Comstock **Lode** turned out to be the largest silver deposit in the history of the United States. In just two years, the mining camp there grew into Virginia City, a rowdy town of 15,000. Today, Virginia City is a small town in the state of Nevada.

Today, Denver has more than 500,000 people.

Primary Source

Mark Twain began his career as a writer in Virginia City, Nevada, when he was 27 years old. He called it "the 'livest' town, for its age and population, that America had ever produced." In his book *Roughing It*, Twain remembered Virginia City this way:

"The sidewalks swarmed with people— to such an extent, indeed, that it was generally no easy matter to stem the human tide.... Money was as plenty as dust; every individual considered himself wealthy, and a melancholy countenance was nowhere to be seen. There were military companies, fire companies, brass bands, banks, hotels, theatres, 'hurdy-gurdy houses,' wide-open gambling palaces, political pow-wows, civic processions, street fights, murders, inquests, riots, a whiskey mill every fifteen steps ... and some talk of building a church."

Virginia City, Nevada, in 1866

A wagon train of settlers crosses the Great Plains in 1870.

"Free land!" Those two words had the same magic sound as "gold!" The words made people who hoped for a better life look to the West. In 1862, President Abraham Lincoln signed the Homestead Act. The act offered 160 acres of free land in the West to any men, widows, and single women who wanted it.

Immigrants could claim 160 acres if they planned to become citizens. If a person lived on the land and farmed at least part of it for five years, it was his or hers to keep. With new farmland becoming scarce in the East, many people thought it was time to go West.

The Homestead Act looked like a great offer for a family who wanted a fresh start. But when some families sat down to plan the move, they saw problems. They would need a wagon to carry their belongings West and oxen or horses to pull it. They would need building materials for a house and barn. And they would need money for seeds and food to last until their first harvest. Setting up a farm in the West could be very costly, but help did become available for the would-be farmers. And it came from a surprising place—the railroads.

✔ **POINT**

Talk It Over

Reread pages 10 and 11. Why did the railroad companies want people to move West? Discuss your answer with a partner.

farming the Great Plains, 1870

Towns grew along new railroad lines.

On May 10, 1869, one last spike was hammered into one last rail. Finally, the transcontinental railroad was complete. It was no longer necessary to cross the West on horseback, by wagon, or on foot. The railroad ran from Omaha, Nebraska, to Sacramento, California. Six other railroad lines in the West soon linked up with it.

The railroad companies encouraged people to settle in the West. Why? First, more settlers meant more freight. Everything from new plows to stoves would travel by rail. So would the mail, and goods such as sugar and coffee. The railroads would also carry farmers' crops and ranchers' cattle to markets in the Midwest and the East. Second, the government had given the railroad companies large pieces of land for every mile of track laid, and the companies wanted to sell that land at a profit.

In the West, railroad companies owned miles of land on both sides of the tracks. If you were a farmer, would it make sense to buy land from a railroad company when you could get it free? Strange as it seems, it would make sense. If you bought land from a railroad company, it might throw in some extras. It might transport your household belongings for free. If you were coming from Europe, the railroad company might get you a cheaper boat ticket. It might even provide temporary shelter while you built your new house.

Still, many settlers continued to take advantage of the government's offer of free land.

Oklahoma land rush, October 22, 1889

In 1889, the land that is today the western part of the state of Oklahoma was settled overnight in a great land rush. For many years, citizens had wanted to settle on that land, even though the U.S. government had already promised it to Native Americans. The government finally gave in to the settlers' demands. On April 22, 1889, at the sound of a bugle, some 60,000 people sprang from a starting line drawn across land in Indian Territory. By nightfall, all the land was claimed. Guthrie and Oklahoma City became bustling cities of 10,000 people in a single day.

Settlers rush to get land in Kansas in 1893.

It's a Fact

How did Oklahoma get its nickname, the Sooner State? In the land rush, some settlers didn't wait for the bugle signal. They rushed in and made their claims "sooner" than others.

By 1900, about 7 million people, including freed slaves and Civil War veterans, owned farms or worked on farms in the West. Yet only about 600,000 of them had benefited from the Homestead Act. Most settlers bought their land from railroads or private real-estate dealers.

It's a Fact

The railroad was a matter of life and death for a town. If the railroad passed through or near a town, that town would probably prosper. A town that was bypassed would probably fail. If you were an official who planned railroad routes, you had a risky job. People might bribe you to run the line near their town. If you chose another place, watch out! Losing the railroad was enough to make some folks violent.

Engineers plan a railroad line in 1888.

Living on the Great Plains

Imagine that your family came to the West to farm. The North-Western Railway sold your parents land in the Great Plains. The railroad's agents gave your parents information on the newest ways to grow wheat and corn. But there was plenty they didn't tell them.

They didn't tell them to expect this:
- – 40° Fahrenheit in winter
- 118° Fahrenheit in summer
- blizzards
- flash floods
- hailstorms
- not enough rain
- dust storms
- prairie fires
- hard soil
- no trees
- swarms of grasshoppers
- rattlesnakes

Primary Source

Suppose you lived in Europe in the late 1800s. You might see a poster like this in your own language in a barbershop window: OWN A FARM NOW! CHEAP LAND! COME TO NEBRASKA! The railroad companies in the West sent hundreds of agents all over Europe to sell land. They offered special deals on tickets. They painted a rosy picture of farm life in the West. And their methods worked. Many of the millions of immigrants to the United States settled in the West as farmers.

The Great Plains had the best farmland in the West, but farming it was not easy. The long roots of the prairie grass made it difficult to break up the soil. Too often, a **drought**, or long period of time with no rain, wiped out an entire crop. Hot winds burned the crops and blew away the dry topsoil. Sometimes, swarms of grasshoppers ate the crops. Many settlers gave up on the Great Plains and left.

a dust storm on the Great Plains

a sod house on the Great Plains

Those settlers who stayed found ways to meet the challenges of the Great Plains. Since few trees grew on the prairies, settlers made houses out of **sod** rather than wood. Sod was soil held tightly together by long roots of grass. The settlers cut slabs of sod and used them like bricks.

Farmers imported hardy kinds of wheat from northern Europe that could withstand the fierce winds of the plains.

New plows with steel tips could cut through the sod so the wheat could be planted. With new machines for harvesting and threshing, the farmers could plant more acres. Since wood was in short supply, farmers built fences with a new invention called "barbed wire." These spiked metal fences kept grazing cattle and sheep from trampling their crops.

The farmers on the Great Plains were tough. They had to be. Because of their hard work, farm production kept growing. Between 1860 and 1900, the amount of land in the United States that was farmed grew by 430 million acres. At the same time, the number of hours needed to produce one acre of wheat fell from 61 to 3.

Before they were settled, most people thought of the Great Plains as a wasteland. But those days were over. The Plains had become a "breadbasket" for the world.

a North Dakota farm
around 1890

Life was hard for the women in the West.

Farm women in the West helped plant and harvest crops, as did farm women in the East. They did the same kinds of daily household chores. But life was harder for the western women. Most settlers couldn't carry all their household items on the long trek west. And they couldn't afford to buy replacements for everything they left behind. They had to be creative. No stove? Then learn to cook and bake over an open fire. No rolling pin? Roll out your biscuits with an empty bottle. No broom? Gather some sagebrush to sweep the floor. No kerosene for lamps? Use melted lard, or animal fat, in a shallow dish and a wick made out of twisted rag.

It's a Fact

Just about everyone in the West—men, women, and children—needed to know how to ride a horse. In an emergency, they might have to ride miles to the nearest town to get a doctor.

Settlers faced another big challenge: prairie fires. Lightning might spark a fire in the tall, dry grasses. A strong wind could quickly whip a fire out of control. One word described most prairie fires: *disaster.*

a prairie fire, 1891

Primary Source

Gro Svendsen (SVEHN-suhn), a woman settler, wrote about prairie fires in an 1863 letter: "It is a strange and terrible sight to see all the fields a sea of fire. Quite often the scorching flames sweep everything along in their path—people, cattle, hay, fences. In dry weather with a strong wind the fire will race faster than the speediest horse. . . ."

cowhands in Colorado, 1883

The story of life on the Great Plains would not be complete without talking about cattle. Between the mid-1860s and mid-1880s, the cattle industry was "king" in much of the West. Huge herds grazed on the open range, or prairie. Beginning in the southern plains, the cattle industry stretched north into Kansas and then across eastern parts of Colorado, Wyoming, and Montana.

Powerful ranchers—the cattle barons—clashed with sheepherders. There wasn't enough grass to support both sheep and cattle, so the cattle barons wanted sheep off the open range. In Wyoming, ranchers dynamited entire herds of sheep or drove them off cliffs. Sometimes **feuds**, or fights, between families turned into cattle-sheep wars.

Fences contributed to the end of the open range.

The cattle boom did not last for long. Some ranchers did not have enough land to feed the number of cattle they had. Many cattle died in a terrible blizzard during the winter of 1886–1887.

Open grazing lands dwindled further as cattle ranchers, sheepherders, and farmers fenced in their lands. The days of the open range came to an end.

✓POINT

Read More About It

Read these Navigators™ books to learn more about settling the West:

Cowhands and Cattle Trails by Margaret C. Moran

Gold Rush! by Eric Kraft

The Transcontinental Railroad by Eric Kraft

Native Americans Betrayed

Many different Native American nations lived in the West when settlers started arriving in 1861. Nations such as the Cheyenne (shy-EHN), Lakota (luh-KOH-tuh), Arapaho (uh-RAP-uh-hoh), and Comanche (koh-MAN-chee) lived on the Great Plains. They hunted buffalo on horseback. These native people were fierce warriors and talented horsemen. They inspired fear in their enemies but also admiration for their skills and spirit.

three Native American chiefs of the Piegan (pee-GAN) nation

In 1865, more than 12 million buffalo grazed on the Great Plains. It seemed that there were enough to last forever. Then easterners took a fancy to buffalo hides. Professional hunters saw that they could make money shooting buffalo. They could sell the hides at a profit in the East. Hunters shot the huge animals, skinned them, and hauled the hides to the nearest railroad line.

Other hunters killed buffalo for food for the U.S. Army and the crews building the railroads. Hunters left the plains covered with the remains of dead buffalo.

It's a Fact

Unbelievable as it seems, in only about 25 years, hunters reduced the number of buffalo from 12 million to less than 1,000.

Hunters shot millions of buffalo.

It's a Fact

The Plains Indians needed the buffalo. Their food, clothing, teepees, and fuel came from the buffalo. The bones were turned into cups, spoons, knives, and arrowheads. Sinews (parts of the body that connect muscles to bones) were made into thread and bow strings.

Year after year, the Plains Indians lost their buffalo. They also lost their land to miners, ranchers, and farmers. The United States government forced the Plains Indians to move to **reservations**. Reservations were areas that were set aside for Native Americans to live on. But the reservations were too small for good hunting. Many Native Americans went hungry or even starved. Thousands died of diseases such as smallpox and measles. Before the arrival of the settlers, these diseases were unknown to the Plains Indians.

Plains Indians were forced to live on reservations.

Battle of Little Bighorn, June 25, 1876

The Plains Indians were able to fight off the U.S. Army longer and more successfully than Native American nations in other areas.

They fought hundreds of battles with the U.S. Army. One of the best known is the Battle of Little Bighorn. In 1875, a gold strike brought thousands of prospectors streaming into the Black Hills of the Dakota Territory. This was sacred land to the Lakota nation. The U.S. government had signed a treaty giving the hills to the Lakota forever. But the U.S. Army did not keep its promise.

The Lakota and Cheyenne joined forces to fight back. In June 1876, Lieutenant Colonel George Armstrong Custer and his troops were on a scouting mission.

They found a huge force of Lakota and Cheyenne encamped at the Little Bighorn River in Montana. Colonel Custer and his men attacked, and the Lakota and Cheyenne killed them all. The U.S. Army took revenge. By the next winter, they had killed many Lakota and Cheyenne and forced the rest to surrender.

By 1890, the Plains Indians had turned to a new religious ritual called the Ghost Dance. They believed it would make all the white people disappear from the plains. They hoped it would bring back their dead people and the buffalo. The U.S. Army thought the dance meant that more war was coming. The army captured and killed the great Lakota leader, Sitting Bull.

Colonel Custer and his men take their disastrous final stand against the Lakota and Cheyenne at the Battle of Little Bighorn.

His followers were pursued and also caught. In a final explosion of violence, the army fired on their prisoners at camp at Wounded Knee Creek. More than 200 Lakota men, women, and children were killed. The blood of the dead stained the snow deep red. The last hope of the Plains Indians died at Wounded Knee.

More than 200 Lakota died at Wounded Knee, South Dakota.

✷ THEY MADE A DIFFERENCE ✷

Susan La Flesche Picotte was a member of the Omaha nation. She was the first Native American woman to become a doctor.

Picotte was born in 1865 on the Omaha reservation in Nebraska. Her father, chief of the Omaha nation, believed that education was necessary to be successful in America. After Susan attended schools on the reservation, her father sent her to schools in the East. In 1889, she graduated from medical school at the top of her class. From about 1891 to 1894, Picotte was the head doctor on the reservation. Later, she established a hospital there. The hospital was named for Picotte after she died in 1915.

Conclusion

The period from 1862 to 1890 was an astonishing time in the West. Think about all the things that happened. The first transcontinental railroad was built. Towns and cities sprang up in the blink of an eye. Prairies became fields of wheat and corn. A thriving cattle industry was born. However, not all the changes were positive. The great buffalo herds were slaughtered. And the Native Americans of the West lost their lands. Many lost their lives.

Few American stories have sparked people's imaginations more than the stories of the West. Stories of settlers' adventures, Native Americans on horseback, gold rushes, and cattle wars are popular around the world. The history of the West is one of the greatest stories ever told.

The stories of the West—part history, part legend—recall a time, long ago, when the West was "won." They make it sound fun, adventurous, and exciting. They seldom stress the hardships and the struggles of settling the West.

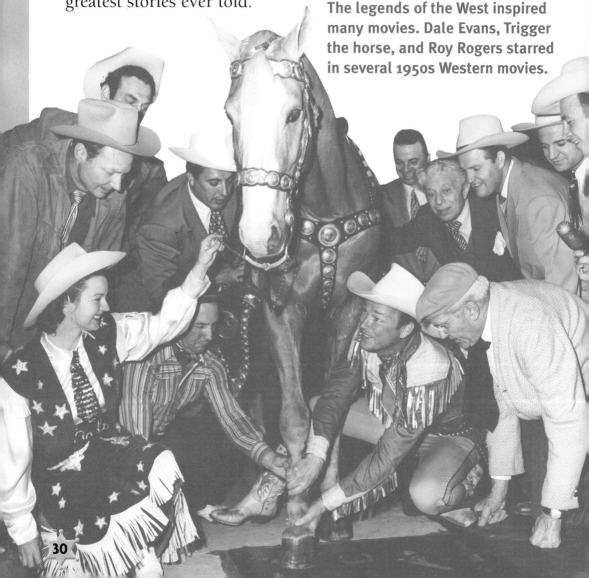

The legends of the West inspired many movies. Dale Evans, Trigger the horse, and Roy Rogers starred in several 1950s Western movies.

Glossary

drought
(DROWT) a long period of dryness that causes damage, such as harm to crops (page 16)

feud
(FYOOD) a long-lasting quarrel, often between two families (page 21)

lode
(LOHD) a large deposit of something valuable, such as gold or silver (page 7)

prairie
(PRAYR-ee) a treeless, grass-covered plain (page 3)

reservation
(reh-zer-VAY-shun) an area of land set aside by the U.S. government that Native Americans were forced to live on (page 25)

rush
(RUHSH) a large movement of people to a new place in search of something such as gold or land (page 6)

settle
(SEH-tul) to set up a home or community (page 3)

sod
(SAWD) soil held tightly together by long roots of grass (page 17)

strike
(STRIGHK) the discovery of something valuable, for example, gold, silver, or oil (page 4)

territory
(TEH-rih-tor-ee) a geographical area (page 2)

Index